1 MONTH OF
FREE
READING

at

www.ForgottenBooks.com

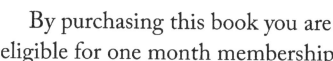

By purchasing this book you are eligible for one month membership to ForgottenBooks.com, giving you unlimited access to our entire collection of over 1,000,000 titles via our web site and mobile apps.

To claim your free month visit:

www.forgottenbooks.com/free949483

ISBN 978-0-260-45743-1
PIBN 10949483

This book is a reproduction of an important historical work. Forgotten Books uses state-of-the-art technology to digitally reconstruct the work, preserving the original format whilst repairing imperfections present in the aged copy. In rare cases, an imperfection in the original, such as a blemish or missing page, may be replicated in our edition. We do, however, repair the vast majority of imperfections successfully; any imperfections that remain are intentionally left to preserve the state of such historical works.

Historic, archived document

Do not assume content reflects current
scientific knowledge, policies, or practice

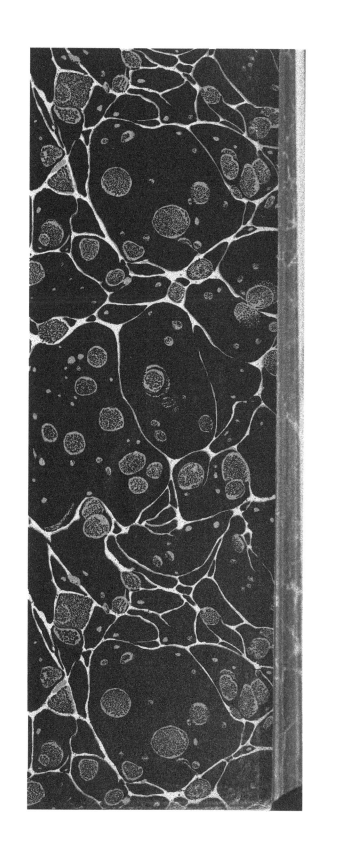

S. R. A.—Fed. Hort. Bd. 64.   Issue September 13, 1919.

United States Department o   griculture,

FEDERAL HORTICULTURAL BOARD.

C. L. Marlatt, *Chairman;* W. A. Orton, Geo. B. Sudworth, W. D. Hunter, Karl F. Kellerman; R. C. Althouse, *Secretary.*

SERVICE AND REGULATORY ANNOUNCEMENTS.

JUNE–JULY, 1919.

CONTENTS.

QUARANTINE ON ACCOUNT OF FLAG SMUT AND TAKE-ALL DISEASES. NOTICE OF QUARANTINE NO. 39 (WITH REGULATIONS).

[Effective on and after Aug. 15, 1919.]

The fact has been determined by the Secretary of Agriculture, and notice is hereby given, that two dangerous plant diseases, namely, flag smut (*Urocystis tritici*) and take-all (*Ophiobolus graminis*), not heretofore widely prevalent or distributed 'within and throughout the United States, exist in Australia; that flag smut is known to exist also in India and Japan and take-all in Italy, France, Germany, Belgium, Great Britain, Ireland, and Brazil, as well as Australia. The flag-smut disease affects wheat (*Triticum*) and the take-all disease affects wheat (*Triticum*), oats (*Avena*), barley (*Hordeum*), rye (*Secale*), and rice (*Oryza*).

Now, therefore, I, Clarence Ousley, Acting Secretary of Agriculture, under the authority conferred by the act of Congress approved August 20, 1912, known as the plant quarantine act (37 Stat., 315), do hereby declare that it is necessary, in order to prevent the further introduction into the United States of the dangerous plant diseases mentioned above, to forbid absolutely, effective August 15, 1919, the importation into the United States of seed or paddy rice (*Oryza* spp.) and of all species and varieties of wheat (*Triticum* spp.), oats (*Avena* spp.), barley (*Hordeum* spp.), and rye (*Secale* spp.) in the raw or uncleaned or unprocessed state, from the countries and localities above mentioned, except on compliance with the following regulations:

REGULATIONS GOVERNING ENTRY OF WHEAT, OATS, BARLEY, AND RYE.

REGULATION 1.—*Applications for permits.*

Persons contemplating the importation of wheat, oats, barley, or rye into the United States shall, before same is shipped, make application for a permit on forms provided for that purpose to the Secretary of Agriculture, Washington, D. C., stating the name and address of the exporter, the country and locality where grown, the port of departure, the proposed port of entry, and the name and address of the importer or of the broker in the United States to whom the permit should be sent.

REGULATION 2.—*Permits for entry.*

On approval of an application a permit will be issued in quadruplicate. One copy will be furnished to the applicant for presentation to the customs officer at the port of entry, one copy will be mailed to the collector at the port of entry, one copy to the inspector of the Department of Agriculture at the port of entry, and the fourth will be filed with the application. All permits will be valid from date of issuance until revoked. Permits will be issued for the ports of Seattle and San Francisco and such other ports as may be specified in the permits.

REGULATION 3.—*Marking as condition of entry.*

Every bag or other container of wheat, oats, barley, or rye offered for entry shall be plainly marked with such numbers or marks as will make it easily possible to associate the bags or containers with a particular importation.

REGULATION 4.—*Notice of arrival by permittee.*

Immediately upon the arrival of the wheat, oats, barley, or rye at the port of entry the permittee shall submit in duplicate notice to the Secretary of Agriculture through the collector of customs on forms provided for that purpose, stating the number of the permit, the number of bags or other containers of the cereal included in the shipment, the bag or container numbers or marks, the country and locality where grown, the name and address of the exporter or foreign shipper, the port of departure, date of arrival, the name of the ship or vessel, and the designation of the dock where the cereal is to be landed.

REGULATION 5.—*Condition of entry.*

The wheat, oats, barley, or rye shall not be removed from the port of entry nor shall any bag or other container thereof be broken or opened except for the purpose of sterilization until a written notice is given to the collector of customs by an inspector of the Department of Agriculture that the wheat, oats, barley, or rye has been properly sterilized and released for entry without further restrictions so far as the jurisdiction of the Department of Agriculture extends thereto. All apparatus and methods for accomplishing such sterilization must be satisfactory to the Federal Horticultural Board. The cereal imported will be delivered to the permittee for sterilization upon the filing with the collector of customs of a bond in the amount of five thousand ($5,000) dollars or in an amount equal to the invoice value of the cereal if such value be less than five thousand ($5,000) dollars, with approved sureties, conditioned upon sterilization of the cereal under the supervision and to the satisfaction of an inspector of the Department of Agriculture and upon the redelivery of the cereal to the collector of customs within 40 days from the arrival of the same at the port of entry: *Provided,* That in the case of wheat, oats, barley, or rye imported for milling purposes, the bran or products containing bran and screenings only shall be subject to sterilization.

REGULATION 6.—*Cancellation of permits for violation of regulations.*

Permits may be canceled and further permits refused for the importation of any of the products covered by this quarantine on the failure of the permittee to give any notice required by these rules and regulations, or for the giving of a false or incomplete notice, or the mislabeling of any shipment with the intent to evade any provision of the plant quarantine act or any of the regulations thereunder.

These regulations shall not apply to husked or polished rice imported for food purposes.

The foregoing regulations are adopted, effective on and after August 15, 1919.

Done in the District of Columbia this 2d day of July, 1919.

Witness my hand and the seal of the United States Department of Agriculture.

[SEAL.]

CLARENCE OUSLEY,
Acting Secretary of Agriculture.

FORMS REQUIRED BY THE FOREGOING REGULATIONS.

(These will be furnished on application.)

UNITED STATES DEPARTMENT OF AGRICULTURE.

FEDERAL HORTICULTURAL BOARD.

WASHINGTON, D. C.

APPLICATION FOR PERMIT TO IMPORT WHEAT, OATS, BARLEY, AND RYE.

_____; 19___

To the FEDERAL HORTICULTURAL BOARD,
Washington, D. C.

SIRS: A permit is requested for the importation of the cereals described below:

_____

_____

Exporter _____
              (Name.)   (Address.)

Country where grown_____

Locality where grown_____

Port of departure_____

Name and address of person (either applicant or his agent or broker) to whom

permit should be mailed_____

If this application is approved and a permit issued, none of the above-described cereals will be moved from the port of entry except in compliance with the rules and regulations of the Secretary of Agriculture governing the importation of wheat, oats, barley, and rye into the United States.

     Very respectfully,

_____
            (Name of applicant.)

_____
            (Address.)

UNITED STATES DEPARTMENT OF AGRICULTURE.

FEDERAL HORTICULTURAL BOARD.

WASHINGTON, D. C.

PERMIT TO IMPORT WHEAT, OATS, BARLEY, AND RYE.

(Valid until revoked.)

_____, 19___

To the Collector of Customs, _____

You are hereby authorized, so far as the jurisdiction of the Department of Agriculture is concerned, to permit the entry, under the plant quarantine act approved August 20, 1912, of the cereals described herein, in accordance with the rules and regulations prescribed under Notice of Quarantine No. 39, on account of flag smut and take-all diseases of grains, effective on and after August 15, 1919.

Exact description of cereals to be imported:

Exporter _____
          (Name.)   (Address.)

Country and locality where grown_____

Importer _____
           (Name.)   (Address.)

    Respectfully,

                               D. F. HOUSTON,
                           Secretary of Agriculture.

  Countersigned:

               (Chairman of board.)

            In Charge of Entry of Plants and
            Plant Products Under Restriction.

          UNITED STATES DEPARTMENT OF AGRICUTURE,
             FEDERAL HORTICULTURAL BOARD,
               WASHINGTON, D. C.

                       Customs Entry No. _____

IMPORTER'S OR BROKER'S REPORT OF ARRIVAL OF WHEAT, OATS, BARLEY, AND RYE
                   AT PORT OF ENTRY.

    In accordance with the plant quarantine act of August 20, 1912, and regulation 4 of the regulations governing the entry of wheat, oats, barley, and rye promulgated July 2, 1919, the information provided for in this blank must be given in duplicate by the permittee or his representative to the Secretary of Agriculture, Washington, D. C., through the collector of customs at the port of entry designated in the permit, immediately upon the arrival of the wheat, oats, barley, and rye.

                                 D. F. HOUSTON,
                             Secretary of Agriculture.

              ---------------------------------, 19__.

The FEDERAL HORTICULTURAL BOARD,
           Washington, D. C.

    The following cereals offered for entry under Permit No. _____ shipped from _____,
                    (Port of departure.)

consigned to_____
          (Name of importer or broker at port of entry.)

arrived _____, 19___, on_____
                (Name of vessel and steamship line.)

dock_____.

    Country and locality where grown_____

    Foreign shipper_____
                  (Name and address.)

Kind of cereal.	Quantity.	Numbers or marks.
....	....	....
....	....	....
....	....	....
....	....	....

    Respectfully,

          (Name of importer or broker at port of entry.)

                     (Address.)

LILY OF THE VALLEY CLUMPS MUST BE FREE FROM SAND, SOIL, OR EARTH.

JULY 14, 1919.

Regulation 3 of the rules and regulations supplemental to Quarantine 37 provides that the nursery stock and other plants and seeds specifically mentioned therein, including lily of the valley, may be imported under permit when free from sand, soil, or earth.

Since lily of the valley clumps practically always carry more or less sand, soil, or earth, importers are warned that such clumps imported under the provisions of this regulation will be thoroughly inspected upon arrival in this country and if sand, soil, or earth is found adhering to the roots the shipment may be refused entry.

It is suggested that lily of the valley be imported in the form of pips rather than clumps, and that they be thoroughly cleaned by washing so as to insure their freedom from sand, soil, or earth.

C. L. MARLATT,
Chairman of Board.

EXPLANATION OF PROVISIONS FOR ENTRY OF PLANT NOVELTIES AND PROPAGATING STOCK UNDER QUARANTINE NO. 37.

JULY 28, 1919.

Regulation 14 of the regulations relative to the importation of nursery stock and other plants and seeds has been revised and reissued. In its new form it is essentially an interpretation of the old regulation 14 rather than an enlargement of powers under the quarantine, inasmuch as the regulation, as worded in the quarantine as originally issued, was intended to cover exactly what is now more clearly stated in the new regulation. This regulation provides for the importation under a special permit from the Secretary of Agriculture of limited quantities of otherwise prohibited stock for the purpose of keeping the country supplied with new varieties of plants and stock for propagation purposes not available in the United States. This amendment, however, does not apply to a few plants which have been specifically prohibited entry under other quarantines, as, for example, pines, *Ribes* and *Grossularia* from certain countries, and citrus, banana, and bamboo stock.

The following explanations of regulation 14 are given to indicate the limitations under this regulation and the procedure to be followed in making importations of the two classes of plants specified, namely, new varieties and necessary propagating stock.

The expression "*New varieties*" is understood to mean plant novelties, that is, new horticultural or floricultural creations or new discoveries.

"*Necessary propagating stock*" is understood to mean stock of old or standard varieties imported for the multiplication of the plants in question as a nursery or florist enterprise as distinguished from importations for immediate or ultimate sale of the stocks actually imported, and such importations will be restricted to stocks which are not available in this country in adequate quantities.

The expression "*Limited quantities*" used in regulation 14 is understood to mean with respect both to new varieties and to standard stocks, such quantities as will supply reasonable needs for the establishment of reproduction plantings which may be thereafter independent of foreign supplies.

There is no limitation as to the number of permits for different plants or classes of plants under regulation 14 which an individual may request, but the applications will all be passed upon both as to necessity for the particular importation and as to the quantity adequate for the purpose intended, by experts of the department, for the information of the board prior to the issuance of the permits.

All importations under regulation 14 must be made under special permits through the Office of Foreign Seed and Plant Introduction of the Department of Agriculture but for the use of the individual importer. The importer will be required to meet all entry, transportation, and freight-handling charges. The department will make no charge for inspection and supervision. The necessary procedure for making such importations is as follows:

1. The Federal Horticultural Board will supply, on request, an application blank upon which request may be made for a special permit to import. This application embodies an agreement on the part of the importer that if the imported material is found on examination by an inspector of the Department of Agriculture to be so infested or infected with insects or disease that it can not be adequately safeguarded it may be destroyed, and such destruction will not be made the basis of a claim against the Department of Agriculture for damages. The application must be accompanied by a statement certifying that the plants to be imported are novelties, or if standard varieties of foreign plants that stocks in adequate quantities for their propagation are not available in this country, and that in either case they are to be imported for the establishment of reproduction plantings and not for immediate or ultimate sale of the stocks actually imported. In exceptional cases the importation of novelties may be made for personal use but not for sale. The application must also give the name and address of the exporter, country, and locality where the stock was grown, the name and address of the importer and the name and address of the nursery or other establishment in which the plants are to be reproduced on release.

2. If the permit is issued, the applicant will be furnished shipping instructions and shipping tags, to be forwarded with his order to the exporter. The plants will, in consequence, be addressed in bond to the U. S. Department of Agriculture, Bureau of Plant Industry, Washington, D. C., United States of America, and indorsed, "Foreign Seed and Plant Introduction, for (insert name of importer)," and arrangements must be made with some responsible agency in Washington for the clearance of the plants when received through the customhouse at Georgetown, D. C., together with the payment of all charges involved.

3. Upon clearance through the Georgetown customhouse the material will be turned over to the Office of Foreign Seed and Plant Introduction by the authorized agent of the importer and in the specially equipped inspection houses and under expert

care as to the welfare of the plants be carefully examined by inspectors of the Federal Horticultural Board. If found free from dangerous insects or diseases, the shipment will be immediately and carefully repacked and forwarded by express, charges collect, to the importer.

4. Should importers request permits covering the importation of larger quantities of propagating or other stock under regulation 14 than can be housed and cared for in the inspection houses of this department, and should such request be approved such importers may be required to provide local storage in Washington for such material during the period of detention for examination and, if necessary, disinfection. Where possible the original containers will be employed for repacking the material, but the importer will be required to meet the cost of such repacking and of new containers when such are necessary. Small shipments which can be easily handled will be repacked without charge. For the present the board will undertake, on request, to provide for such storage and repacking but reserves the right to require the importer to provide for such work through his own agents.

5. Cleaning and disinfection will occur for slight infestation, but should the material be found to be so infected or infested with either disease or insects that it can not be so adequately safeguarded it will either be destroyed or, when possible and desirable, returned to the point of origin.

C. L. MARLATT,
Chairman of Board.

NOTICE OF PUBLIC HEARING OF PROPOSED QUARANTINE ON ACCOUNT OF THE FLAG SMUT AND TAKE-ALL DISEASES OF GRAINS AND THE WHEAT NEMATODE OR EELWORM DISEASE.

JUNE 18, 1919.

The Secretary of Agriculture has information that three dangerous diseases, namely, flag smut (*Urocystis tritici*), take-all (*Ophiobolus graminis*), and the wheat nematode or eelworm disease (*Tylenchus tritici*), not heretofore widely prevalent or distributed within and throughout the United States, have been determined as existing in this country as follows: (1) Flag smut in Illinois, (2) take-all in Indiana and Illinois, and (3) the wheat nematode or eelworm disease in the States of Virginia, West Virginia, and Georgia. The flag smut affects wheat; the take-all affects wheat, oats, barley, and rye; and the wheat nematode or eelworm disease affects wheat, oats, rye, spelt, and emmer.

It appears necessary, therefore, to consider the advisability of quarantining the States above named in accordance with the plant quarantine act of August 20, 1912 (37 Stat., 315), as amended by act of Congress approved March 4, 1917 (39 Stat., 1134, 1165), and of restricting or prohibiting the movement from the States of Indiana and Illinois of wheat, oats, barley, and rye; and from the States of Virginia, West Virginia, and Georgia of wheat, oats, rye, spelt, and emmer into other States, Territories, and districts.

Notice is therefore hereby given that a public hearing will be held at the Department of Agriculture, Washington, D. C., Room 11, Federal Horticultural Board, at 10 o'clock a. m., July 15, 1919, in order that any person interested in the proposed quarantine may appear and be heard either in person or by attorney.

The flag smut affects the leaf blades, leaf sheaths, stems, and sometimes the spikes of wheat. Usually every shoot is affected, the leaves wither, and the spike is frequently replaced by a mass of twisted leaves. The spores are carried on the seed and live over in the soil. In portions of Australia the losses from this disease run from one-tenth to one-half of the crop.

The take-all disease, known also as whitehead or footrot, attacks the roots and the base of the plants, rotting the roots and blackening the base of the stem. Young wheat plants speedily wither and die; older ones may survive but rarely produce grain. Heavy losses have been sustained in all countries where this disease occurs.

The nematode or eelworm disease is caused by a tiny worm which attacks the young seedlings, causing a decided rolling, wrinkling, twisting or other distortion of the leaves. The plants may die, or if they mature, they always produce dwarfed diseased heads bearing hard black galls filled with eelworm larvæ. When the galls are sown with the wheat the nematodes escape and infect the seedlings. Losses of from 50 to 80 per cent have been caused in some fields by this organism.

THE FLAG SMUT, TAKE-ALL, AND WHEAT NEMATODE SITUATION.

The public hearing on account of the flag smut and take-all diseases and the wheat nematode or eelworm disease of grains held at the Department of Agriculture July 15, 1919, was largely attended. All of the States mentioned in the notice of hearing with the exception of West Virginia were well represented by State officials and by members of grain dealers' and millers' associations. The subjects of the hearing were thoroughly discussed, and as a result of the information obtained, which indicated that the States concerned had ample legal powers to take the necessary steps to control the diseases and to prevent the interstate movement of diseased products, and had, in the case of Indiana, already instituted control measures, the department deemed it unnecessary to establish a Federal quarantine at this time.

No quarantine will be recommended by the department with respect to the nematode or eelworm disease of cereals. It was brought out at the hearing that this disease has been in this country for a considerable period without spreading rapidly, and it appeared that the States particularly interested were in a position to undertake effective control work by means of rotation of crops and by the use of clean seed.

The following press notice in regard to flag smut and take-all was issued by the Office of Information of the United States Department of Agriculture July 21, 1919:

SEES ERADICATION OF NEW WHEAT DISEASES.

Department of Agriculture Believes Flag Smut and Take-All Are Now Under Control.

WASHINGTON, D. C., *July 21, 1919.*—Indications are that the two dreaded foreign foes of wheat, flag smut and take-all, will not become widespread in the United States. The United States Department of Agriculture announces that the two States where these diseases appeared, Indiana and Illinois, have taken steps that will prevent the spread of the diseases from the infected fields and that should wipe out in a few years the infection in fields where it exists.

Indiana officials came to the recent hearing in Washington with adequate safeguards already placed. Shortly after the hearing, Illinois established similar safeguards. All the infected wheat in both States is under control and will be disinfected before any use whatever is made of it. All straw and stubble are to be burned, thrashing machines are to be thoroughly disinfected, and no wheat is to be grown in infected areas for several years.

BUT FIGHT IS NOT OVER.

Under these conditions full confidence is felt that neither of the diseases will spread from the diseased areas in Illinois and Indiana. That does not mean, however, that the fight against flag smut and take-all is over. It is possible that one or both of the diseases exist this year in places where they have not been recognized. There is, however, no great probability that this is true. The Department of Agriculture and its cooperating agencies have been diligently on the lookout for these two diseases all summer and have found no evidences of them except in the two areas. Both flag smut and take-all occur in Illinois and only take-all in Indiana. The experts, however, realize the possibility that some infested spots may have escaped observation, and it would not be surprising if diseased fields are found elsewhere next spring.

In the meantime there will be no let-up in the work of preventing either of the diseases from getting a real foothold anywhere in the United States. The Federal department is working with the authorities of Illinois and Indiana, giving them every possible aid. Its pathologists are energetically studying the diseases, and its representatives are searching the country over to make certain whether or not there are other infested areas, and to see that effective measures of control are available if any such areas are discovered.

PROMPT STATE ACTION PREVENTS QUARANTINE.

The cooperation of State authorities is essential in order to prevent hardship if further infestations should be discovered. Only the prompt action of Indiana and Illinois prevented the placing of a quarantine against all the wheat in those States, a measure which would have meant hardship, not only to all the wheat growers in the two States, but to dealers, millers, and consumers. Even prompter State action will be desirable if either of the diseases is found later to exist in any other State.

Neither of these diseases is likely to find its way into the country again from outside sources. The Department of Agriculture has established quarantine regulations against all the rest of the world in which either of the diseases exists. No small grain can come in for any purpose unless it has been thoroughly sterilized with steam heat. It is the purpose of the department, say its officials, to make the clean-up of these plant plagues as thorough and as prompt as it did the foot-and-mouth disease of animals a few years ago.

THE STATE OF ARKANSAS PROVIDES FOR INSPECTION OF MAIL SHIPMENTS OF PLANTS AND PLANT PRODUCTS.

OFFICE THIRD ASSISTANT POSTMASTER GENERAL,
Washington, June 12, 1919.

The State of Arkansas will establish on July 1, 1919, places for the terminal inspection of plants and plant products under the provisions of the act of March 4, 1915, embodied in section 478¼, Postal Laws and Regulations, appearing on page 49 of the May, 1915, Supplement to the Postal Guide.

All postmasters are therefore informed that packages containing plants or plant products addressed to places in the State of Arkansas may be accepted for mailing only when plainly marked so that the contents may be readily ascertained by an inspection of the outside thereof. The law makes the failure so to mark such parcels an offense punishable by a fine of not more than $100.

The plants and plant products subject to terminal inspection in the State of Arkansas are described as follows:

"All florists' stock, trees, shrubs, vines, cuttings, grafts, scions, buds, fruit pits and other seeds of fruits and ornametal trees or shrubs, and other plants and plant products in the raw or unmanufactured state, except vegetable and flower seeds: *Provided,* That this list of plants and plant products shall not apply to plants and plant products shipped under the certificate of the Federal Horticultural Board of the United States Department of Agriculture."

Postmasters within the State of Arkansas shall be governed strictly by the provisions of paragraphs 3, 4, 5, and 6, section 478¼, Postal Laws and Regulations, in the treatment of all packages addressed for delivery at their offices containing any of the plants or plant products above described as subject to terminal inspection.

July 1, 1919, inspection service will be inaugurated and maintained at Little Rock and Fayetteville, Ark., and on and after that date all postmasters in that State shall, after receiving the required postage therefor, under the provisions of section 478¼, Postal Laws and Regulations, send to the nearest inspection point each package containing plants or plant products, subject to terminal inspection.

Owing to the perishable character of plants and plant products, the packages containing such matter must be given prompt attention.

Any failure of compliance with the foregoing instructions or with the provisions of section 478¼, Postal Laws and Regulations, coming to the attention of any postmaster should be reported to the Third Assistant Postmaster General, Division of Classification.

[Reprinted from June supplement to the United States Official Postal Guide.]

RESTRICTIONS ON THE MAILING OF CERTAIN PLANTS AND PLANT PRODUCTS, AND STONE OR QUARRY PRODUCTS, FROM PORTIONS OF THE STATES OF MAINE, NEW HAMPSHIRE, MASSACHUSETTS, RHODE ISLAND, AND CONNECTICUT ON ACCOUNT OF THE GIPSY MOTH AND THE BROWN-TAIL MOTH.

JULY 25, 1919.

THE POSTMASTER.

Inclosed for your information and guidance, under the provisions of section 478, Postal Laws and Regulations, is a copy of revised Quarantine Order No. 33, with regulations issued by the Secretary of Agriculture, effective July 1, 1919, quarantining certain areas in the States of Maine, New Hampshire, Massachusetts, Rhode Island, and Connecticut, for the brown-tail moth and the gipsy moth.

The coniferous trees, or parts thereof, and decorative plants; the forest-plant products; the field-grown florists' stock, trees, shrubs, vines, cuttings, and other plants and plant products for planting or propagation; the stone or quarry products; and the deciduous trees and shrubs, or such parts thereof as bear leaves, the movement of which is restricted by the quarantine order above referred to, may be accepted for mailing only under the conditions prescribed by that order. Such of these articles as are required by the quarantine order to be inspected by the Department of Agriculture may be accepted for mailing only when accompanied with a certificate of a representative of that department to the effect that they have been inspected and found free from the brown-tail moth or gipsy moth, or both, as the case may be.

Maps showing the areas quarantined on account of the gipsy moth and brown-tail moth can be obtained on application to Mr. A. F. Burgess, agent, United States Department of Agriculture, 964 Main Street, Melrose Highlands, Massachusetts.

These instructions supersede those contained in the circular letter of this office dated July 25, 1918.

A. M. DOCKERY,
Third Assistant Postmaster General.

LIST OF CURRENT QUARANTINE AND OTHER RESTRICTIVE ORDERS.

QUARANTINE ORDERS.

The numbers assigned to these quarantines indicate merely the chronological order of issuance of both domestic and foreign quarantines in one numerical series. The quarantine numbers missing in this list are quarantines which have either been superseded or revoked. For convenience of reference these quarantines are here classified as domestic and foreign.

DOMESTIC QUARANTINES.

Date palms.—Quarantine No. 6: Regulates the interstate movement of date palms or date-palm offshoots from Riverside County, Calif., east of the San Bernardino meridian; Imperial County, Calif.; Yuma, Maricopa, and Pinal Counties, Ariz.; and Webb County, Tex.; on account of the Parlatoria scale (*Parlatoria blanchardi*) and the Phoenicococcus scale (*Phoenicococcus marlatti*).

Cotton seed and cottonseed hulls.—Quarantine No. 9: Prohibits the importation of cotton seed and cottonseed hulls from the Territory of Hawaii on account of the pink bollworm.

Hawaiian fruits.—Quarantine No. 13, revised: Prohibits or regulates the importation from Hawaii of all fruits and vegetables, in the natural or raw state, on account of the Mediterranean fruit fly and the melon fly.

Sugar cane.—Quarantine No. 16: Prohibits the importation from Hawaii and Porto Rico of living canes of sugar cane, or cuttings or parts thereof, on account of certain injurious insects and fungous diseases.

Cotton.—Quarantine No. 23, revised: Regulates the movement of cotton from Hawaii to the continental United States, on account of the pink bollworm.

Five-leafed pines, Ribes and Grossularia.—Quarantine No. 26, as amended: Prohibits the interstate movement of five-leafed pines, currant and gooseberry plants from all States east of and including the States of Minnesota, Iowa, Missouri, Arkansas, and Louisiana to points outside of this area; prohibits, further, (1) the interstate movement of five-leafed pines and black-currant plants to points outside the area comprising the States of Maine, New Hampshire, Vermont, Massachusetts, Rhode Island, Connecticut, and New York, and (2) to protect the State of New York, the movement from the New England States, on account of the white-pine blister rust.

Sweet potato and yam.—Quarantine No. 30: Prohibits the movement from the Territories of Hawaii and Porto Rico into or through any other Territory, State, or District of the United States of all varieties of sweet potatoes and yams (*Ipomoea batatas* and *Dioscorea* spp.), regardless of the use for which the same are intended, on account of the sweet-potato weevil (*Cylas formicarius*) and the sweet-potato scarabee (*Euscepes batatæ*).

Banana plants.—Quarantine No. 32: Prohibits the movement from the Territories of Hawaii and Porto Rico into or through any other Territory, State, or District of the United States of any species or variety of banana plants (*Musa* spp.), regardless of the use for which the same are intended, on account of two injurious weevils, *Rhabdocnemis obscurus* and *Metamasius hemipterus*.

Gipsy moth and brown-tail moth.—Quarantine No. 33, revised: Regulates the movement interstate to any point outside of the quarantined towns and territory, or from points in the generally infested area to points in the lightly infested area, of stone or quarry products, and of the plants and the plant products listed therein. The quarantine covers portions of the States of Maine, New Hampshire, Massachusetts, Rhode Island, and Connecticut.

Japanese beetle.—Quarantine No. 35: Regulates the movement interstate to any point outside of the townships of Delran, Chester, and Cinnaminson, Burlington County, N. J., of green corn, commonly called sweet or sugar corn, on account of the Japanese beetle (*Popillia japonica*).

European corn borer.—Quarantine No. 36: Prohibits the movement interstate to any point outside of the quarantined area of corn fodder or cornstalks whether used for packing or otherwise, green sweet corn, roasting ears, corn on the cob, and corn cobs, on account of the European corn borer (*Pyrausta nubilalis*).

Black stem rust.—Quarantine No. 38: Prohibits the movement interstate to any point outside of the quarantined area of the common barberry and its horticultural varieties, as well as certain other species of Berberis and Mahonia, on account of the black stem rust of wheat, oats, barley, rye, and many wild and cultivated grasses.

FOREIGN QUARANTINES.

Irish potato.—Quarantine No. 3: Prohibits the importation of the common or Irish potato from Newfoundland; the islands of St. Pierre and Miquelon; Great Britain, including England, Scotland, Wales, and Ireland; Germany; and Austria-Hungary, on account of the disease known as potato wart.

Mexican fruits.—Quarantine No. 5, as amended: Prohibits the importation of oranges, sweet limes, grapefruit, mangoes, achras sapotes, peaches, guavas, and plums from the Republic of Mexico, on account of the Mexican fruit fly.

Five-leafed pines, Ribes, and Grossularia.—Quarantine No. 7, as amended: Prohibits the importation from each and every country of Europe and Asia, and from the Dominion of Canada and Newfoundland, of all five-leafed pines and all species and varieties of the genera *Ribes* and *Grossularia*, on account of the white-pine blister rust.

Cotton seed and cottonseed hulls.—Quarantine No. 8, as amended: Prohibits the importation from any foreign locality and country, excepting only the locality of the Imperial Valley, in the State of Lower California, Mexico, of cotton seed (including seed cotton) of all species and varieties, and cottonseed hulls, on account of the pink bollworm. Cotton and cotton seed from the Imperial Valley may be entered under permit and regulation.

Seeds of avocado or alligator pear.—Quarantine No. 12: Prohibits the importation from Mexico and the countries of Central America of the seeds of the avocado or alligator pear, on account of the avocado weevil.

Sugar cane.—Quarantine No. 15: Prohibits the importation from all foreign countries of living canes of sugar cane, or cuttings or parts thereof, on account of certain injurious insects and fungous diseases. There are no restrictions on the entry of such materials into Hawaii and Porto Rico.

Citrus nursery stock.—Quarantine No. 19: Prohibits the importation from all foreign localities and countries of all citrus nursery stock, including buds, scions, and seeds, on account of the citrus canker and other dangerous citrus diseases. The term "citrus," as used in this quarantine, includes all plants belonging to the subfamily or tribe *Citratæ*.

European pines.—Quarantine No. 20: Prohibits, on account of the European pineshoot moth (*Evetria buoliana*), the importation from all European countries and localities of all pines not already excluded by Quarantine No. 7.

Indian corn or maize and related plants.—Quarantine No. 24, as amended: Prohibits the importation from southeastern Asia (including India, Siam, Indo-China, and China), Malayan Archipelago, Australia, New Zealand, Oceania, Philippine Islands, Formosa, Japan, and adjacent islands, in the raw or unmanufactured state, of seed and all other portions of Indian corn or maize (*Zea mays* L.), and the closely related plants, including all species of Teosinte (*Euchlaena*), Job's tears (*Coix*), *Polytoca*, *Chionachne*, and *Sclerachne*, on account of the downy mildews and *Physoderma* diseases of Indian corn, except that Indian corn or maize may be imported on compliance with the conditions prescribed in the regulations of the Secretary of Agriculture.

Citrus fruit.—Quarantine No. 28: Prohibits the importation from eastern and southeastern Asia (including India, Siam, Indo-China, and China), the Malayan Archipelago, the Philippine Islands, Oceania (except Australia, Tasmania, and New Zealand), Japan (including Formosa and other islands adjacent to Japan), and the Union of South Africa of all species and varieties of citrus fruits, on account of citrus canker, except that oranges of the mandarin class (including satsuma and tangerine varieties) may be imported on compliance with the conditions prescribed in the regulations of the Secretary of Agriculture.

Sweet potato and yam.—Quarantine No. 29: Prohibits the importation for any purpose of any variety of sweet potatoes or yams (*Ipomoea batatas* and *Dioscorea* spp.) from all foreign countries and localities, on account of the sweet potato weevils (*Cylas* spp.) and the sweet potato scarabee (*Euscepes batatae*).

Banana plants.—Quarantine No. 31: Prohibits the importation for any purpose of any species or variety of banana plants (*Musa* spp.), or portions thereof, from all foreign countries and localities, on account of the banana root borer (*Cosmopolites sordidus*).

Bamboo.—Quarantine No. 34: Prohibits the importation for any purpose of any variety of bamboo seed, plants, or cuttings thereof capable of propagation, including all genera and species of the tribe *Bambuseae*, from all foreign countries and localities, on account of dangerous plant diseases, including the bamboo smut (*Ustilago shiraiana*). This quarantine order does not apply to bamboo timber consisting of the mature dried culms or canes which are imported for fishing rods, furniture making, or other purposes, or to any kind of article manufactured from bamboo, or to bamboo shoots cooked or otherwise preserved.

Nursery stock, plants, and seeds.—Quarantine No. 37, as amended, with regulations (effective on and after June 1, 1919) : Prohibits the importations of nursery stock and other plants and seeds from all foreign countries and localities on account of certain injurious insects and fungus diseases, except as provided in the regulations. Under this quarantine the following plants and plant products may be imported without restriction: Fruits, vegetables, cereals, and other plant products imported for medicinal, food, or manufacturing purposes, and field, vegetable, and flower seeds. The entry of the following plants for propagation is permitted under restriction: Lily bulbs, lily of the valley, narcissus, hyacinths, tulips, and crocus; stocks, cuttings, scions, and buds of fruits; rose stocks, including manetti, multiflora, brier rose, and rosa rugosa; nuts, including palm seeds; seeds of fruit, forest, ornamental, and shade trees; seeds of deciduous and evergreen ornamental shrubs, and seeds of hardy perennial plants.

Flag smut and take-all.—Quarantine No. 39, with regulations (effective on and after August 15, 1919) : Prohibits the importation of seed or paddy rice from Australia, India, Japan, Italy, France, Germany, Belgium, Great Britain, Ireland, and Brazil on account of two dangerous plant diseases known as flag smut (*Urocystis tritici*) and take-all (*Ophiobolus graminis*). Wheat, oats, barley, and rye may be imported from the countries named only on compliance with the conditions prescribed in the regulations of the Secretary of Agriculture.

OTHER RESTRICTIVE ORDERS.

The regulation of the entry of nursery stock from foreign countries into the United States was specifically provided for in the plant-quarantine act. The act further provides for the similar regulation of any other class of plants or plant products when the need therefor shall be determined. The entry of the plants and plant products listed below has been brought under such regulation:

Nursery stock.—Nursery stock is entered under regulations requiring a permit, foreign certification and marking, reporting arrival and distribution, and inspection at destination. The term "nursery stock" includes all field-grown florists' stock, trees, shrubs, vines, cuttings, grafts, scions, buds, fruit pits and other seeds of fruit and ornamental trees or shrubs, and other plants and plant products for propagation, except field, vegetable, and flower seeds, bedding plants, and other herbaceous plants, bulbs, and roots. (These regulations will remain in force until June 1, 1919. See Quarantine No. 37.)

Irish potatoes.—The importation of Irish potatoes is prohibited altogether from the countries enumerated in the potato quarantine. Potatoes may be admitted from other foreign countries in accordance with the order of December 22, 1913, bringing the entry of potatoes under restriction on account of injurious potato diseases and insect pests. The following countries have qualified for the importation of potatoes under the regulations issued under said order: Denmark, Holland, Belgium, Cuba, Bermuda, and the Dominion of Canada. The regulations issued under this order have been amended so as to permit, free of any restrictions whatsoever under the plant-quarantine act, the importation of potatoes from any foreign country into the Territories of Porto Rico and Hawaii for local use only and from the Dominion of Canada and Bermuda into the United States or any of its Territories or Districts.

Avocado, or alligator pear.—The order of February 27, 1914, prohibits the importation from Mexico and the countries of Central America of the fruits of the avocado, or alligator pear, except under permit and in accordance with the other provisions of the regulations issued under said order, on account of the avocado weevil. Entry is permitted only through the port of New York and is limited to the large, thick-skinned variety of the avocado. The importation of the small, purple, thin-skinned variety of the fruit of the avocado and of avocado nursery stock under 18 months of age is prohibited.

Cotton.—The order of April 27, 1915, prohibits the importation of cotton from all foreign countries and localities, except under permit and in accordance with the other provisions of the regulations issued under said order, on account of injurious insects, including the pink bollworm. These regulations apply in part to cotton grown in and imported from the Imperial Valley, in the State of Lower California, in Mexico.

Corn.—The order of March 1, 1917 (Amendment No. 1, with Regulations, to Notice of Quarantine No. 24), prohibits the importation of Indian corn or maize in the raw or unmanufactured state from the countries and localities listed in Notice of Quarantine No. 24, except under permit and in accordance with the other provisions of the regulations issued under said order, on account of injurious diseases of Indian corn.

Cottonseed products.—The order of June 23, 1917, prohibits the importation of cottonseed cake, meal, and all other cottonseed products, except oil, from all foreign countries, and a second order of June 23, 1917, prohibits the importation of cottonseed oil from Mexico except under permit and in accordance with the other provisions of the regulations issued under said orders, on account of injurious insects, including the pink bollworm.

Citrus fruits.—The order of June 27, 1917 (Notice of Quarantine No. 28, with Regulations), prohibits the importation from the countries and localities listed therein of all species and varieties of citrus fruits, excepting only oranges of the mandarin class (including satsuma and tangerine varieties), on account of the citrus-canker disease. Oranges of the mandarin class (including satsuma and tangerine varieties) may be imported under permit and in accordance with the other provisions of the regulations issued under said order.

WASHINGTON : GOVERNMENT PRINTING OFFICE : 1919